# NEW ZEALAND LANDSCAPES

## PHOTOGRAPHY BY ANDRIS APSE

### INTRODUCTION BY ANDY DENNIS

craig potton publishing

DEDICATION

To the memory of my mother Kamilla

ACKNOWLEDGEMENTS

There are many people whose generous assistance over the last twenty years has enabled me to
collect thousands of images throughout New Zealand. This book features approximately 100 of these images. Many
of the photographs would have been difficult if not impossible to achieve without the generous
assistance of the following people: Alan Bond, Richard Hayes, Tim Innes, Lou Sanson, Dave Saxton, Jeff Shanks,
Ken Tustin and Simon Williamson.

First published in 1994, revised in 2006. This reprint 2010.
Craig Potton Publishing, 98 Vickerman Street, PO Box 555, Nelson, New Zealand
www.craigpotton.co.nz

Photography: Andris Apse
Introduction: Andy Dennis

© Photography: Andris Apse

ISBN 978-1-877333-32-3

Scanning by Image Centre, Auckland, New Zealand
Printed in China by Midas Printing International Ltd

# Contents

INTRODUCTION   6

THE COASTLINE   14

LOWLAND WILDERNESS   34

PASTORAL LAND   46

HIGH COUNTRY   70

MOUNTAINS   92

ISLANDS   112

# INTRODUCTION

I don't remember exactly when it was that I first became aware of a photographer called Andris Apse, perhaps because he is a modest and private man and seemingly not given to proclaiming his talents with an excessive amount of song and dance. It might have been in the glossy tourist publications, which regularly featured his work during the 1980s, or in one of those omnibus volumes about New Zealand landscapes that also emerged during those same years – like Kenneth Cumberland's *Landmarks* or Reader's Digest's *Wild New Zealand*. At all events, by the beginning of the 1990s I had begun soliciting a few photographs from him each year for a range of wild places calendars I was involved in helping to produce. And each time a bundle of Apse transparencies arrived in our Nelson office I felt a real hankering for the wild country from which his images were drawn. I felt too that the impact of these photographs was very much enhanced by the way he consistently seemed able to capture beautiful or dramatic light. And there was clearly also something unusually satisfying about lingering over images of landscapes that had been composed in panoramic format. As far as I was aware, Andris was one of very few landscape photographers in New Zealand who were then working principally in this extended format, and it seemed to me to provide him with a distinct advantage over others working in this same field.

Photography first became a major component of Andris's destiny in 1963, when the then young Forest Service woodsman landed himself a job with the Forest and Range Experiment Station in Rangiora near Christchurch. Here he began a phase of his life that took him on surveys to the vast and remote wilderness of Fiordland, and brought him into regular contact with the renowned Forest Service photographer John Johns. On these survey trips to Fiordland, and to the North Island's Kaweka Ranges, he quickly fell in love with New Zealand's unspoiled natural wilderness, which seemed to him an infinitely preferable environment to production forests planted in straight rows. Fiordland especially seemed wonderfully wild and empty, and he was totally overwhelmed by its beauty and scenic grandeur. He soon found himself wishing he had some means of recording these magnificent vistas – and more or less decided there and then to try and become a landscape photographer. That this was not an impossible dream was evident to him in the work of John Johns, whose black and white photographs of Fiordland reminded him of aspects of Chinese painting in the way that they seemed at times to reach beyond mere physical portrayal of forests, fiords and mountains towards some deeper awareness of the region's intrinsic character. Accordingly, Andris was soon the proud owner of the first of his many cameras (in this case a basic Agfa "Clack") which over the next few years he carried with him everywhere, gradually learning that there was a great deal more to the art of landscape photography than simply pointing his camera at some inspiring piece of scenery and pressing the shutter button!

This pioneer period in Andris's life came to an end in 1970 when Rangiora chemist Neil Harrison helped him to buy a local photographic business that by chance had come up for sale. Thus he was able to embark on a career as a professional photographer, albeit one that was dominated in the early years not by wilderness landscapes but by a more mundane diet of portrait, passport and wedding photography. Trips to the wilds during these years were few and far between, and instead Andris devoted his energies to building up the business and advancing his knowledge of the properties of light and lenses and film. The bid for freedom from this routine photographic fare was eventually made in 1978 when he plucked up the courage to purchase a Linhof Technorama camera, capable of producing wide format "panoramic" transparencies 6cm in depth by 17cm in length. This was the only camera of its type in New Zealand at the time, and its $5000 price tag was a huge sum for a small-town photographer to contemplate paying for an essential item of photographic equipment, let alone a device as novel (and as radical) as this. Somehow Andris managed to convince the bank that he was the person fated to become its new owner, a decision that in the event, neither had subsequent cause to regret. Indeed, immediately he began exploring its exciting innovative possibilities, Andris realised that here at last was a camera that was perfectly suited to both his own photographic inclinations and to the dimensions of the kind of landscapes that had first enticed him into photography, and to which he had always remained determined to some day devote more time.

The door leading back to landscape work that was pushed ajar by the purchase of the panoramic camera was finally flung wide open in the early 1980s when Andris returned from a wonderful year's travelling through Chile with his young family and decided that the moment had come to devote himself full time to photographing landscapes. If at that time he could have written his own job description it would probably have been as a freelance photographer for *National Geographic* magazine, maintaining a New Zealand base while regularly carrying out assignments elsewhere in the world. But a number of extended solitary photographic trips into remote parts of Fiordland during the early 1980s were enough to convince him that his ambitions could just as easily be fulfilled within New Zealand shores – so much so that a decade later he was even confiding to friends that he would be more than content to spend his next twenty years confined to Fiordland. While this hasn't happened, the deep empathy Andris has long felt for the wilder parts of New Zealand resulted in a move, in 1999, to the coastal village of Okarito in the South Westland glacier country where, even when he is not away with his cameras, glorious panoramas of sea and forest and lofty snow-capped mountains fill his daily horizons.

For 150 years or more, writers, painters and photographers have been drawing attention to the fact that New Zealand as a whole contains a variety of landscapes and scenery unmatched anywhere else in the world, at all events, within such a compact area. In this small country have been gathered together numerous graphic examples of the great earth-shaping processes of tectonic upheaval, volcanic mayhem and massive glaciation. Coupled with factors like 80 million years of isolation from other large land areas and a frequent occurrence of climatic extremes, these processes have resulted in the highest mountains in Australasia, the most accessible glaciers in the world's temperate regions; a huge (upwards of 10,000 kilometres) and wonderfully diverse expanse of coastline; large tracts of virgin rainforest; stark areas of semi-arid terrain, and a liberal sprinkling of highly individual flourishes in things like intriguing areas of karst (or limestone) landscapes and dazzling examples of geothermal creativity. Here too dramatic contrasts abound, often in close proximity – dry eastern areas and a vastly wetter west; gentle plains terminating in abrupt mountain ranges; a subtropical north and a distinctly temperate south; and large areas of essentially untouched natural wilderness giving way, often quite abruptly, to settled landscapes from which all traces of former wildness have frequently been erased. Qualities like these – and this is by no means a comprehensive catalogue – go some way towards explaining how it is that a photographer of Andris's talents and ambition is able to find everything he needs to satisfy his artistic inclinations without feeling the necessity of travelling to distant lands.

There are, in my experience, five principal factors that determine the outcome of any attempt at photographing landscape. These are: the level of the technical understanding and skill in the use of cameras, lenses, filters and film; an eye for both subject matter and for composition; an inspirational feeling for light; a reservoir of patience (and the deeper the better); and, inevitably, some element of luck. With the exception of the last – which, unlike the others, is not wholly in the hands of the photographer – each of these finds ample testimony in the sample of Andris's work that has been included in this collection. Accordingly, they provide a convenient framework for taking a closer look at a few of these photographs, and, through them, at the landscapes Andris is most anxious to photograph and at the way he goes about recording them on film.

In the course of our conversations about photography, I asked Andris at one point whether he ever felt confident that he had secured the kind of image he wanted at the moment the shutter was released, or whether, like most of us, he waits with some misgivings until the film arrives back from the processing laboratory. Without the slightest suggestion of arrogance he replied that he now always knew, even before the shutter was released, what the outcome would be. So well does he understand his cameras, lenses, filters and films, that if he encounters a landscape that he feels is worth photographing he has no doubts at all about his ability to capture it on film, regardless of the technical problems it may happen to present. To be able to do this his equipment bag usually includes at least five different types of transparency film and a range of seven different filters, and it is a measure of his dedication to familiarising himself with these basic tools of his trade that when experimenting with a new type of film he expects it to take him a least a hundred rolls before he can feel completely confident about that film's performance under the range of conditions to which he is likely to subject it. Because film is able to reproduce the effect of natural light only within a very restricted range of conditions, most of the photographs in this collection have been filtered – and in some cases heavily filtered – but his aim in using filters is rarely merely cosmetic enhancement. Rather, it is an endeavour to reproduce the natural qualities of the atmosphere and light that were

OVERLEAF: Kahikatea forest in South Westland beneath
Mt Tasman and Aoraki/Mt Cook (right of centre).

present when the photograph was taken. And it seems to me clear confirmation that Andris is a technician of exceptional skill that in most cases – including those photographs that involve difficult lighting situations – the evidence of his use of filters will not usually be apparent in the great majority of the photographs included in this book.

While Andris is happy enough to take advantage of most modern developments in the manufacture of filters and film, he remains much more of a traditionalist in his choice of cameras. Having at some time in the past experimented with just about every good quality medium-format camera that has been produced and found them wanting – not necessarily because of optical inadequacies, but rather their inability to survive in the kind of conditions he is likely to subject them to – he has now resorted to having his cameras custom-built to suit his own particular needs. Although these unique devices make use of the very best Schneider lenses and other components of similar impeccable credentials, they are, in many respects, the antithesis of the high-tech cameras produced by most modern manufacturers. They have, for example, only manual functions for aperture, shutter speed and focusing. There is no through-the-lens viewing. And there are no electronic aids or computerised brains. They are, in reality, much more akin to the type of cameras people like Ansel Adams were using half a century ago than to the sophisticated devices employed by most modern professional photographers. He is now experimenting with a digital camera but does not consider it able to match the quality of transparencies taken in the 6x12 and 6x17 formats. Even if the quality of a digital image does eventually match that of the panoramic formats, electronic cameras would not survive the harsh weather conditions routinely experienced on prolonged trips to Fiordland.

As well as providing abundant evidence of a high level of technical skill, these photographs also convey, almost invariably, a very satisfying feeling of aesthetic harmony, even when the mood of the landscape – or seascape – is itself far from harmonious. Time and again I have found myself feeling that the arrangement of the various components is wholly appropriate – almost as if Andris has himself been able to stage-manage the construction of the settings to his own specifications. For example, in the winter photograph of the Ahuriri Valley (p.83) I can picture him searching backwards and forwards for hours on a terrace that has provided him with an elevated lookout across the snow-covered valley floor, trying to assemble the intriguing pattern of river meanders and scattered willows into a composition that he feels will do justice to the landscape as he sees it. Again, in the lovely high-country study of Lake Onslow on pages 80 and 81, painstaking selection of his photographic standpoint and a careful choice of lens has given him a landscape in perfect balance, with

gently rolling tussock ridges carrying the viewer through both foreground and background to the cluster of fishing huts on a sunlit promontory in the centre of the picture. Here too, the pattern of cloud and clear sky balance the arrangement of land and lake water, and a subtle interplay of light and shadow seems wholly in keeping with the overall atmosphere of remoteness and tranquillity.

In both these photographs, as indeed in most others in this book, the compositional qualities are, it seems to me, greatly enhanced by the use of panoramic format. In the case of the former the width of the composition has allowed the full sweep of the river meanders to be included in the foreground without the distancing that a wide-angle lens would have produced, while in the latter, one is left with the feeling that nothing has been omitted from the composition that might in some way have furthered the effect. (As a further test of this meticulous attention to composition try cropping either of these photographs, even to a fairly modest degree, and see what you lose as a consequence!) The results can be even more dramatic in the ultra-wide (6x17) compositions, not only in the case of great sweeps of country like the upper Ahuriri Valley at Ben Avon station (pp.84-85), the mountains encircling Lake Wanaka from a winter evening on Roys Peak (pp.98-99), or the aerial overview of the Canterbury Plains (pp.52-53), but also in photographs of more limited physical focus like the sand dunes on Ninety Mile Beach (p.14), drowned willows in Lake Wanaka (p.70) or the forest interior from Fiordland's Wild Natives Valley (pp.36-37). It is perhaps worth adding in this context that although Andris began his experiments in panoramic photography with a 6x17 camera, his present pattern of use tends to favour the "narrower" 6x12 format. Part of the reason for this is undoubtedly the more limited commercial market for ultra-wide transparencies, at least without cropping (which I know he hates to see happen to any of his careful compositions). But I suspect that there are also aesthetic reasons involved in this choice. The 6x12 format seems more akin to normal scope of human vision, and hence the way we would take in a comfortable slice of the landscape if we had been present to observe the actual scene. It also better suits compositions where the main focus of attention runs strongly through the centre of the photograph, as it does, for example, with the golden crescent of South Westland's remote Ohinemaka Beach (pp.16-17), the evening serenity of the glorious summit pyramid of Mt Aspiring (pp.110-111), or the fledgling wandering albatross keeping solitary vigil over the bleak but beautiful landscape of sub-antarctic Adams Island (p.119).

The lighting, of course, also makes an enormous contribution to the total effect of photographs like these, and I can't escape the conclusion that even the most perfect arrangement of terrestrial components will always fail as a photograph if the operator of the elemental switchboard is in an uncooperative mood. What for me provides the main emotional impact of many of these photographs – and, I think lifts a considerable number of them from competently crafted images to landscape photographs of the highest order – is the quality of the light that has been added to the composition. In many instances – like the extraordinary dream-like photograph of a vast sweep of Fiordland mountains from above Breaksea Sound (pp.24-25), the sun-shot farmland and clay cliffs near Kyeburn (pp.48-49), or the wintery high-country scene at the head of Lake Tekapo (pp.86-87) – the qualities of light are so pervasive and powerful that they totally dominate the way we respond to the photograph from the moment we first encounter it. In others, however, the contribution of the lighting may initially be less obvious but is ultimately no less important. It takes a little time, for example, to fully appreciate the contribution made to the cover photograph of the intriguing patchwork of sunlight and shadow and misty veils of ephemeral morning cloud. In the same way, it was, I suspect, the solitary young bird and dramatic ramparts of sea cliffs that initially caught my attention in the Adams Island photograph on p.119. But what brings me back again and again to this particular photograph is the way threatening black clouds hang over the summit of the island, sunlight dances out across much of the sea, and the whole scene in between becomes a pattern of different moods of intimacy and remoteness – or, perhaps, of security and alienation – as the effects of the dramatic lighting interact with the structural elements of the composition.

I must admit, however, that I find it very much easier to say of these photographs simply that they are "beautifully lit" or "dramatically lit" rather than to try and explain in words what is partly (and perhaps at times wholly) an intuitive emotional response. Dawn and dusk photographs by Andris are invariably beautifully lit, as are many of the rural landscapes (both in the intensity of the greens and the patterns of light and shadow), and virtually all of the photographs of indigenous forest interior. Sombre lighting can be beautiful too, conveying a kind of melancholic beauty that is often absent from popular photographic books on "Beautiful New Zealand", examples of which are the lovely atmospheric study of morning cloud rising from Milford Sound (pp.18-19), the brooding coast of Otago Peninsula near Penguin Beach (pp.28-29), or the bleak winter high-country landscape near the head of Lake Tekapo (pp.86-87). Sombre elements too are a major component of several of the more dramatically lit photographs included in this collection, with the drama resulting from the interplay between sombre and radiant light. Striking examples of this include the Breaksea Sound and Kyeburn farmland photographs mentioned above along with the sublime celestial spotlighting of the snowfields at the head of the Fox Glacier in the photograph on pages 108-109.

In the last of these, patches of dramatic light flood down upon an otherwise dark Fox névé during a brief interlude of elemental cooperation in what was otherwise a week of relentless storms – an emphatic reminder, if indeed we need one, that in landscape photography lighting like this is very much a gift from the gods, and one that they do not always appear to dispense in just proportion to those who deserve it most.

A little over a year ago I got up daily in the pre-dawn darkness to set up my camera and tripod overlooking the beautiful beach at Sealers Bay on Codfish Island and waited for a glorious dawn to erupt over the Ruggedy Mountains on nearby Stewart Island. Not an entirely original undertaking, I hasten to add, but rather an attempt to emulate, and perhaps even outdo, the results of a friend's earlier dawn vigils from the same location and at much the same time of year. At times the omens seemed highly favourable as clouds gathered over the Ruggedy summits while still leaving a band of clear sky on the eastern horizon, conditions tailor-made, or so it seemed, for a dazzling southern sunrise. But despite two weeks of patient perseverance, dawn never really managed to happen in the way that I had hoped it might, and my photographic spoils were accordingly never more than modest.

There is, of course, a rich harvest of other sorts to be gleaned from being up before dawn in wild country despite the lack of cooperation from the elements in achieving photographic objectives; but it is unusual for me – a traveller by nature rather than a watcher – to exhibit the degree of patience that Codfish Island prompted, but it is the path that has taken Andris to many of his most widely acclaimed photographs. This is especially true in respect of his outstanding archive of Fiordland landscapes, many of which have resulted from solitary journeys of up to six weeks at a time to remote camps scattered through the fiords, which became an almost annual event for him throughout the 1980s and early 1990s. Again and again on what were effectively photographic pilgrimages, he would return to the same carefully selected locations in the hope that by so doing this vast solitude of mountains and forests and tumbling waters would eventually yield him the kind of bounty he was seeking. Like it so very clearly did in the moss-draped forests along the Wild Natives River at the head of Bligh Sound (pp.36-37). Or the wonderful serenity of the cover photograph, which he managed to obtain only after returning to the same location in the absolute calm of early morning on a dozen or more occasions during the four weeks he was based in the isolated hut at the head of George Sound.

It must, I think, be self-evident that folk who tend to move through country rather than linger for a time in the same place will need to rely more heavily on luck in encountering the concurrence of landscape and light that can result in a good photograph than a patient and meticulous practitioner like Andris. But despite his careful planning, even Andris frequently draws a blank. For example, despite numerous carefully timed visits to Lake Matheson he has yet to come home with the kind of photograph that satisfies his own exacting standards. The composition has given him few problems – indeed the classic view from the western end of the lake is ideally suited to the wide (or even extra-wide) format. His technical skill is certainly not in question. And his planning will, I am certain, have given careful attention to such matters as the season, the time of day, and the content of the latest weather forecasts. But somehow the crucial ingredients of light and mood have never quite managed to cooperate with Andris in the way he has wanted in respect of this classic West Coast panorama of lake and forest and mountains and sky. In much the same vein, his long-held ambition to photograph a fledgling albatross chick on a sub-antarctic island blanketed by winter snow has been foiled by lack of anything more than ephemeral sleety snow on each occasion he has managed to get onto these far-flung southern outliers of New Zealand during the chillier months of the year. This was again his primary objective during three weeks spent on Campbell Island in September 2005, but although he located exactly the kind of composition he needed during his first few days on the island, the fickle weather gods again seemed determined to deny him anything resembling a substantial delivery of snow. Such a snowfall did finally occur on his last night on the island. But with his chosen albatross chick two hours walk from the hut and the only boat for months departing at daybreak he was left with no choice but to pack up his cameras and once again sail away.

Besides reminding us that there will always be some element of landscape photography that remains beyond the control of even the most painstaking practitioner, these two episodes provide further evidence of the lengths to which Andris is prepared to go in pursuit of his photographic objectives. They also help to reinforce my conviction that the photographs assembled here ultimately owe far more to the kind of qualities I have attempted to describe than they do to any mere matter of chance – that is, to the pains Andris has taken to perfect his craft; to the care he invests over the way he fills his frame; to the appreciation he very clearly has of the contribution made by light; and to the huge amount of patience he is obviously prepared to invest in order to get photographs of a standard that he feels does justice both to the landscapes that most inspire him and his own artistic goals. Indeed, the only photograph in this book that is the outcome of a chance encounter rather than of careful planning and patient execution, is the extraordinary overview of dream-like Fiordland mountains on pages 24-25, which he managed to capture only because his close friend and helicopter pilot Alan Bond had arrived unexpectedly the evening before at his remote camp-site in Dusky Sound. And, perhaps even more fortuitously, also because after a "long night" they somehow managed to drag themselves out of their sleeping bags early enough to be hovering high above the entrance to Breaksea Sound when this ethereal winter dawn began to illuminate the glistening fiord, mist-filled valleys, and surrounding maze of seemingly endless shadowy ridges and snowy peaks.

These reflections on patience and luck seem to me an appropriate point to end these introductory remarks and allow the photographs some space to speak for themselves. Perhaps as others work through them they too will be reminded of the years of patience and dedication required to assemble a collection as memorable as this, and of how lucky we are that people exist who are prepared to devote their lives to enabling the rest of us to see, by the simple act of opening a book, what is beautiful and moving about landscapes and light.

Andy Dennis

George Sound, Fiordland National Park.

# THE COASTLINE

Ninety Mile Beach, Northland.

Nugget Point lighthouse and eroded rock stacks at sunrise, Catlins Coast, South Otago.

ABOVE: Franz Josef Glacier and the Southern Alps above
coastal wetland and rimu forest at Five Mile Lagoon,
Westland/Tai Poutini National Park.
RIGHT: Ohinemaka Beach, South Westland.
OVERLEAF: Morning cloud disperses from Milford Sound's
buttresses and Mitre Peak after a southwesterly storm,
Fiordland National Park.

ABOVE: Sealers Beach, south of Puysegur Point, Fiordland National Park.
LEFT: Lake McKerrow drains into Martins Bay, Fiordland National Park.
OVERLEAF: Cape Reinga, Northland, the northernmost point
of the New Zealand mainland.

21

ABOVE: Mitre Peak, Milford Sound, Fiordland National Park.
PREVIOUS PAGE: Breaksea Sound, Fiordland National Park.

Ocean swells erupt spectacularly through blowholes at Punakaiki in Paparoa National Park.

ABOVE: Taiaroa Head lighthouse, Otago Peninsula.
RIGHT: Storm-driven surf surges onto Penguin Beach on the Otago Peninsula.

Port Jackson and Cape Colville on the Coromandel Peninsula, with Great Barrier Island behind.

ABOVE: Hoopers Inlet and Papanui Inlet from Peggys Hill, Otago Peninsula.

OVERLEAF: Awaroa Bay, Abel Tasman National Park.

# LOWLAND WILDERNESS

Coastal forest beneath the Southern Alps near Waiho, South Westland.

ABOVE: Mt Tasman and Aoraki/Mt Cook (right of centre), reflected in Okarito Lagoon, South Westland.

OVERLEAF: Moss-draped ribbonwood forest and blechnum ferns at Kiwi Lake, Wild Natives Valley, Fiordland National Park.

Forest trunks and tree ferns, Breaksea Sound, Fiordland National Park.

Beech forest and ferns growing beside a stream in Preservation Inlet, Fiordland National Park.

ABOVE: Iota Point and Cascade Beach, South Westland.
RIGHT: Mouth of the Waiho River and the Southern Alps, South Westland.

Looking across the Hope Arm of Lake Manapouri, Fiordland National Park.

Mt Taranaki from the Waiwhakaiho River.

Korokoro Falls, Urewera National Park.

Small forest waterfall at the head of George Sound, Fiordland National Park.

# Pastoral Land

Stooked oats on a North Canterbury farm.

ABOVE: Sunrise over farmland in the Geraldine area, South Canterbury.

OVERLEAF: Golden fields and river escarpment near Kyeburn, Central Otago.

Twisted and wind-shorn macrocarpa trees at Pahia on Southland's southern coast.

ABOVE: Ngaranui Station, near Carterton, Wairarapa.

OVERLEAF: The Canterbury Plains and the Rakaia River below the foothills of the Southern Alps.

ABOVE: Hamilton in morning mist from the lower slopes of Mt Pirongia.
RIGHT: Mudstone hill country farmland near Tahora in the
Taumarunui district, King Country.
PREVIOUS PAGE: Sheep flock being herded on undulating downs at
'Woodlands' near Temuka, South Canterbury.

Cape Egmont lighthouse, with Mt Taranaki in the distance.

ABOVE: Vineyard on Waiheke Island.

OVERLEAF: Church, cemetery and barley crop near Taihape, Rangitikei District.

ABOVE: Mt Aspiring/Tititea from the Barrier Range,
Mount Aspiring National Park.
LEFT: Hereford cattle grazing beneath the Southern Alps near Fox Glacier.

ABOVE: Autumn poplars and willows at Macetown, Central Otago.
PREVIOUS PAGE: Farmland near Fairlie showing the Ben McLeod Range, South Canterbury.

ABOVE: Tolaga Bay farmland, East Cape.
OVERLEAF: Bannockburn and the Pisa Range, Central Otago.

# HIGH COUNTRY

Drowned willows in Lake Wanaka, Otago.

ABOVE: High-country cattle muster on Birchwood Station in the upper Dingle Burn, east of Lake Hawea, Central Otago.
OVERLEAF: Tussock and fog in the Matukituki Valley, Otago, with Mt Aspiring/Tititea in the centre.

ABOVE: The summit of Aoraki/Mt Cook.
LEFT: Larch trees in autumn and the Mt Cook massif from
the shores of Lake Pukaki.
OVERLEAF: Stormbound Southern Alps from the head of Lake Tekapo
looking north up the Godley Valley

ABOVE: Fly fishing for trout in the Ahuriri River, Mackenzie Country.

RIGHT: Sunrise at Lake Onslow, east of Roxborough, in Central Otago.

PREVIOUS PAGE: Salmon fisherman in the upper Rakaia River, Canterbury.

Autumn larch trees at Castle Hill, with the Torlesse Range beyond, Canterbury.

ABOVE: The upper Ahuriri Valley after a mid-winter snowfall, Mackenzie Country.
OVERLEAF: Ben Avon Station, upper Ahuriri Valley.

ABOVE: Musterer and dogs on Dalrachney Station, near Lindis Pass, Mackenzie Country.
PREVIOUS PAGE: Lake Tekapo in the Mackenzie Country.

ABOVE: Looking west across Lake Hawea towards Mt Aspiring/Tititea (obscured) and the peaks of Mount Aspiring National Park.

OVERLEAF: Tussockland at Mesopotamia Station, Rangitata River, Canterbury.

# MOUNTAINS

Head of the Fox Glacier, with Mt Tasman and Aoraki/Mt Cook, Westland/ Tai Poutini National Park.

A 'hogsback' storm cloud enshrouds Aoraki/Mt Cook at sunset.

ABOVE: Aerial view looking south along the ranges of the Southern Alps.
RIGHT: Icefall on the upper Fox Glacier, with Mt Douglas and Mt Haidinger
right of centre.

ABOVE: Rocks and tussock at sunset, Hump Ridge, Fiordland National Park.
LEFT: The Red Hills, South Westland.
OVERLEAF: Lake Wanaka and the Southern Alps from Roys Peak.

ABOVE: Winter snowfall on the Craigeburn Range, Canterbury.
LEFT: Looking down on the Route Burn flats from the Routeburn Track after a winter snowfall, Mount Aspiring National Park.

ABOVE: Karangarua Range, Westland/Tai Poutini National Park.
LEFT: Lake Leeb above the Arawhata Valley looking east to the Haast Range, South Westland.

Mt Ngauruhoe and Mt Ruapehu at sunset, Tongariro National Park.

Mt Taranaki reflected in a tarn, Egmont National Park.

Rata in flower in the Copland Valley, Westland/Tai Poutini National Park.

ABOVE: Mt Tasman (centre) and Aoraki/Mt Cook, from a ridge high above the Fox Glacier in Westland/Tai Poutini National Park.

OVERLEAF: Skiers on Fox Glacier, Westland/Tai Poutini National Park.

ABOVE: The Hooker Range above the headwaters of the
Makawhio River (Jacobs River).
RIGHT: Mt Aspiring/Tititea and the Bonar Glacier from the southwest.

# ISLANDS

Sulphur deposits and steaming fumaroles in the White Island crater, Bay of Plenty.

Steam and sulphur vapour from the White Island volcano, Bay of Plenty.

Mason Bay dunelands, Rakiura National Park, Stewart Island.

Tree on a clifftop against a stormy sky, Kahunene, Chatham Islands.

ABOVE: Sooty albatross nesting amongst megaherbs on a rock outcrop above Fly Harbour, Adams Island, Auckland Islands.

PREVIOUS PAGE: Surf at West Ruggedy Beach, Rakiura National Park, Stewart Island, with Codfish Island on the right.

Wandering albatross, Adams Island, Auckland Islands.

Erect-crested penguin colony and rock stack on Antipodes Island, 1000km southeast of New Zealand.